KENN BIVINS

39 LESSONS FOR TEENS

KENN BIVINS

39 LESSONS FOR TEENS

INVISIBLE ENNK PRESS · ATLANTA

All inquiries received at Invisible Ennk Press, P.O. Box 69, Avondale Estates, GA 30002.

First printing, 2019. Published by Invisible Ennk Press

paperback ISBN: 978-1-7333747-2-9
ebook ISBN: 978-1-7333747-3-6

Design by Kenn Bivins

for the 15-year old
version of me

and all teenagers thereafter

I am invisible, understand, simply because people refuse to see me.

– Ralph Ellison, *Invisible Man*

Being a teenager is hard. Hormones, homework, arrogance, inexplicable angst and outside influences are the bane of their existence and can tax your relationship with them. I've been on both sides of that coin, both as a teen and as a dad. I understand.

If you have a teenager in your life, you may benefit from this addendum to what you're already teaching. This is not a comprehensive list, but more so a foundation to build upon.

love and laughter forever,
Kenn Bivins

01

YOU MATTER

You, your voice and your presence matters.
The world has more hope with you in it.

02

DON'T COMPARE YOURSELF TO OTHERS

You'll never discover who you are if you measure your value by the stature of others. Honor who you were meant to be and spend your time celebrating your unique talents, voice, traits and purpose.

03

TAKE YOUR TIME

Childhood is a very short season.
Don't be in such a hurry to grow up.
You have the rest of your life to be an adult.

04

LOVE YOURS

Learn to love the life that you have,
love the person in the mirror and be thankful
for what you already have.

05

THIS IS TEMPORARY

Whatever painful or uncomfortable thing you're dealing with, know that it will eventually pass.

06

ACNE IS NOT FOREVER

One day, your skin will clear up, just as those problems that make you want to run away from your life. It will get better.

07

THE INTERNET IS FOREVER

Nothing lasts forever, but the Internet does.
Be careful of what you post and publicly share.
Even though you may delete it, it will forever reside
on a server or in a database for someone to
someday access.

08

DO SOMETHING TODAY FOR THE FIRST TIME

Trying new things encourages a healthy mindset.

09

CELEBRATE YOURSELF

It doesn't have to be your birthday for you to honor who you are and your accomplishments, big and small.

10

DRINK MORE WATER

Odds are you're probably not drinking enough water to offset the sugary snacks and fried foods you love so much. Drink more water.

11

WASH YOUR FACE

Practicing good hygiene is not only good for your appearance, but it's also important that you present the best version of yourself. Be clean, be neat and don't stink :)

12

WASH YOUR SPACE

A clean body doesn't wear dirty clothes.
By the same token, your environment informs what is in it. The appearance of your environment can affect your mindset.

13

YOUR BODY IS YOUR OWN

No one has authority over your body but you.

14

POVERTY IS OFTEN BORN OF UNPROTECTED PENISES

Becoming a parent prematurely and while you're still a child increases the likelihood of a difficult life - financially and otherwise. If you are having sex, use condoms.

15

WITH SEX COMES RESPONSIBILITY

The only safe sex is no sex. There is a great deal of responsibility that goes with physical intimacy, including the risk of pregnancy, unwanted diseases and emotional insecurity.

16

SEX IS NOT EQUAL TO LOVE

Love is about selfless, mutual respect and wanting what best for one another. Sex, outside of love, is simply for physical satisfaction that more often leads to low self-worth and diminishes self-respect.

17

SAVE SOME

Enjoy life, but don't spend all you have at once.
This is regarding money, time and yourself.

18

SAYING THANK YOU IS NOT THE SAME AS BEING THANKFUL

Say what you feel and feel what you say.

19

SARCASM IS NOT A LANGUAGE

Don't mistake a sense of humor with a form of communication. Sarcasm can be confusing, mocking and insulting to the listener who's not in on the joke. It also weakens communication skills.

20

RESPECT

Command respect from others just as you choose to give respect to them.

21

ADULTS ARE NOT PERFECT

They're human too, just a little bit older. Be patient with them. They're likely doing the best they know.

22

GET TO KNOW YOUR PARENTS

You can discover a lot about yourself by learning who your parents were when they were teenagers.

23

FIND A MENTOR

You will go further and with less frustration by going with someone who has walked the same path before. A mentor is someone who is trusted, mature-minded and a cheerleader all rolled into one. He or she can help you become a better version of yourself.

24

SHOW. DON'T TELL.

Let your verbs be your words.
Don't just talk about it. Be about it.

25

LET YOUR YES BE YES AND YOUR NO BE NO

Keep your word and fulfill your promises.
Don't offera promise that you don't intend to keep.
Follow through.

26

HELP OUT

Don't wait for someone to ask for your help. If you see something that you can assist with, just do it. The feeling that results from helping others is invaluable.

27

LEARN HOW TO COUNT

Make a difference that is. Find your purpose and flourish there.

28

EVERYONE YOU WILL MEET WILL KNOW SOMETHING YOU DON'T

Approach others with a sense of wonder, respect and curiosity.

29

YOU DON'T KNOW IT ALL

No matter how smart you are, you will always have something to learn. Don't be arrogant with the knowledge and expertise that you do have.

30

IN FIVE YEARS, WHAT HAPPENS IN HIGH SCHOOL WON'T MATTER

What you're stressing about today
won't matter so much tomorrow.

31

STUDY. PREPARE. PLAN.

Always. In school and in life.

32

A JOB IS FOR LOOSE CHANGE

Work hard, but be aware that there is more to life.

33

A CAREER IS FOR LIFE CHANGE

Invest in working hard at something that you love and therein, you might find both purpose and happiness.

34

SOMEONE DOES UNDERSTAND YOU

You're not the only one going through
what you're going through.

You are not alone. You are not the only one.

35

DEPRESSION AND ANGER SHOULD BE EXPRESSED

Don't be ashamed of your feelings. You have the right to them. Write, draw, sing, play or do whatever constructive thing to cope. But above all, talk to someone.When we're sad or angry, we don't think clearly. Get help.

36

SING, DANCE AND PLAY AIR GUITAR

Have fun. Life is short. Make your own kind of music.

37

LISTEN

The world around you is saying so much.
Listen to what is said as well as what isn't.

38

WATCH

There is so much to see. Pay attention to the little things and the behaviors in the space you occupy.

39

SEEK GOD ALWAYS

Whether you know God or not,
continually seek for answers.

You are the dream. Discover the dreamer.

I am the dad I always wanted. My own father was absent, but I refused to let that color the type of influence I would have on my sons and with my goddaughter.

The teenager phase of parenting can be tough. In the next few bonus pages, I want to share some observations that may give you, as a parent, strength that I lovingly call "**4 Lessons for Former Teens**."

BONUS 1

BE PATIENT

You weren't always the most respectful.
You didn't always listen. Once upon a time, you may have even been self-centered.

But then you grew up.
It will happen with your teen, as well.

BONUS 2

BE THERE

They may act as if they don't care about what you have to say or your presence, but they do.
Be physically and emotionally present because they will indeed need you to be.

BONUS 3

BE SMARTER

Your child navigates in spaces that you need to be knowledgeable of. The whole world has access to them through digital technology. Don't be afraid of it.

BONUS 4

BE PATIENT

~ ~ ~ ~ ~

And I'll repeat it because hormones, arrogance, inexplicable angst and outside influences will tax your relationship with your child.

This is a phase. They will eventually grow past it. Be patient.

THE SIGNIFICANCE OF 39

You may be wondering, "What's the deal with 39? Why wasn't this book called 101 Lessons or something like that? 39 is just odd."

Well, let me explain. Years ago when I was blogging regularly, I went through what I lovingly regard as my "list phase." Lists are an amazing way to quantify accomplishments, goals, things to do, groceries, etc.

I ran across an internet challenge to detail random things about myself and this turned into a post titled "99 Things." This was my inaugural list, but it got so much feedback that I challenged myself further to write another list and then another, each one being a quantity divisible by 3 and ending in 9. Apparently, I was also into numeric themes.

Fun fact: June is my favorite month. It's a reflective time because so many events happen that month that are significant to me. Father's Day, being among those events, prompted me to write a list from a dad's perspective. My numbering pattern had landed on 39 around the time this list was conjured and thus was born ***39 Lessons for Boys***.

Numerology indicates that 39 is associated with direction and guidance in discovering life's purpose. While I didn't know this at the time of the original writing, it's kismet how that worked out.

It's amazing to me how what seems so random can actually have meaning after all. So there you have it – the significance of 39.

love and laughter forever,
kenn

A STUDY GUIDE OF 21

What are lessons without study guides, right?
The following is a bonus list of lessons that I gleaned from the internet for the sake of open discussion and interpretation with your child.

These snippets can be savored by adults too, as reminders or principles to consider. Enjoy!

1. YOU ARE BEAUTIFUL.

2. LOVE YOURSELF.

3. TALK TO GOD DAILY.

4. ASK TOO MANY QUESTIONS.

5. IT'S OKAY TO NOT HAVE ALL THE ANSWERS.

6. SOME TIMES, BABY STEPS.

7. CHOOSE LIFE EVERYDAY.

8. LIFE DOESN'T COME IN FANCY WRAPPING,
BUT IT'S STILL A GIFT.

9. DON'T DO ANYTHING YOU DON'T WANT TO DO.

10. DON'T APOLOGIZE FOR WHO YOU ARE.

11. FRAME DECISIONS WITH, "WILL THIS MATTER TOMORROW? IN FIVE YEARS?"

12. DO WHAT YOU SAY.

13. HOWEVER GOOD OR BAD THE SITUATION IS, IT WILL/ALWAYS/CHANGE.

14. DON'T RUSH IT. UNLESS YOU'RE RACING.

15. YOUR BODY ISN'T WHO YOU ARE. YOUR CHARACTER IS.

16. STOP OVERTHINKING.

17. CRYING WITH SOMEONE IS BETTER THAN HEALING ALONE.

18. NOTHING LASTS FOREVER.

19. BEFORE YOU DO GREAT THINGS, DO THE SMALL THINGS WELL.

20. GOD LOVES YOU BECAUSE OF WHO GOD IS, NOT BECAUSE OF ANYTHING THAT YOU'VE DONE OR DIDN'T DO.

21. STAY CURIOUS.

Thank you for taking the time to read and consider this very important book. It's meant to be read multiple times and shared with others. And by share, I mean tell people where and how to get their own copy or gift them one. Just between you and me, I've learned not to loan books because I never get them back ☺

39 Lessons for Boys, ***39 Lessons for Girls*** and ***39 Lessons for Black Boys & Girls*** are also available. They make great companions to this book and look great together on a bookshelf or coffee table.

love and laughter forever,
Kenn Bivins

OTHER BOOKS BY KENN BIVINS

39 LESSONS FOR BLACK BOYS & GIRLS

39 LESSONS FOR BOYS

39 LESSONS FOR GIRLS

THE WEDDING & DISASTER OF FELONA MABEL

PIOUS

Made in the USA
Coppell, TX
07 July 2020

30264978R00066